TRAILBLAZERS of the MODERN WORLD

Mar 24, 2004

ELEANOR ROOSEVELT

By Jonatha A. Brown

WORLD ALMANAC® LIBRARY

Please visit our web site at: www.worldalmanaclibrary.com
For a free color catalog describing World Almanac® Library's list
of high-quality books and multimedia programs, call 1-800-848-2928 (USA)
or 1-800-387-3178 (Canada). World Almanac® Library's fax: (414) 332-3567.

Library of Congress Cataloging-in-Publication Data

Brown, Jonatha A.
    Eleanor Roosevelt / by Jonatha A. Brown.
      p. cm. — (Trailblazers of the modern world)
    Includes bibliographical references and index.
    Summary: A biography of the First Lady who, despite her shyness, followed her conscience
and devoted her life to helping others and working for peace.
    ISBN 0-8368-5079-3 (lib. bdg.)
    ISBN 0-8368-5239-7 (softcover)
    1. Roosevelt, Eleanor, 1884-1962—Juvenile literature. 2. Presidents' spouses—United States—
Biography—Juvenile literature. [1. Roosevelt, Eleanor, 1884-1962. 2. First ladies. 3. Women—
Biography.] I. Title. II. Series.
    E807.1.R48B76   2002
    973.917'092—dc21
    [B]   2002022701

This edition first published in 2002 by
World Almanac® Library
330 West Olive Street, Suite 100
Milwaukee, WI 53212 USA

This edition © 2002 by World Almanac® Library.

Project editor: Mark J. Sachner
Design and page production: Scott M. Krall
Photo research: Diane Laska-Swanke
Editor: Alan Wachtel
Indexer: Walter Kronenberg
Production direction: Susan Ashley

Photo credits: © AP/Wide World Photos: 4, 16, 23, 25, 32; © Baldwin H. Ward & Kathryn C. Ward/CORBIS: 5 top;
© Bettmann/CORBIS: 6, 7 top, 9 top, 20 both, 21, 22 top, 24, 26, 30, 34, 35 both; © CORBIS: 10, 27 top, 33 top;
Courtesy of Franklin D. Roosevelt Library: cover, 5 bottom, 7 bottom, 8, 9 bottom, 11, 15, 17, 18 bottom, 19,
22 bottom, 27 bottom, 28, 33 bottom, 36, 38, 39, 40 top, 41, 42; © Hulton Archive/Getty Images: 12 both, 40 bottom,
43; © Hulton-Deutsch Collection/CORBIS: 14; © James Marshall/CORBIS: 18 top; © Seattle Post-Intelligencer
Collection; Museum of History & Industry/CORBIS: 29

Printed in the United States of America

1 2 3 4 5 6 7 8 9 06 05 04 03 02

TABLE of CONTENTS

Words that appear in the glossary are printed in **boldface**
type the first time they occur in the text.

CHAPTER 1

A GREAT REFORMER

Brought up in a wealthy family and married to the president of the United States, Eleanor Roosevelt could have led a comfortable life filled with parties and entertainment. Instead she chose to work hard—so hard that most people could not keep up with her—trying to help some of the poorest, most neglected people in America and working for peace and **human rights** around the world.

As first lady, Eleanor Roosevelt promoted interest in social issues through her television and radio broadcasts, newspaper columns, magazine articles, and personal appearances.

AN ADVOCATE FOR WOMEN

In the early 1900s, women did not have the same rights as men under the law. They did not have the same opportunity to get an education or a good job, and they could not vote. If a woman wanted to work or had to support herself, there were few laws protecting her. She was paid far less than a man for doing the same job, she could be fired if a man wanted her position, and she often had to work very long hours if she wanted to keep her job.

Eleanor Roosevelt fought to change this situation. Coming onto the political scene just after women received the right to vote in 1920, she urged women to learn about issues that affected their lives and speak out for themselves. She also encouraged women to work and argued for changes that would improve their living and working conditions. Through her efforts, she became a role model for women everywhere who wanted to be productive and independent.

In the early 1900s, many women worked at menial jobs in crowded, unsanitary conditions and earned very low wages.

A VOICE FOR RACIAL EQUALITY AND INTEGRATION

The lives of black Americans were even harder than those of working women. Discriminated against on the job, in society, and in schools, most African Americans lived in poverty. Although they had the right to vote, they had little representation in government and their needs were usually ignored.

Mrs. Roosevelt, who lived through the two world wars, thought it was wrong for Americans to fight oppression around the world while tolerating it at home. Acting on that belief, she encouraged the president to include people of all races in federal assistance programs. She also worked for equal opportunity and racial **integration** in the U.S. armed forces and championed legislation that would protect the **civil rights** of African Americans. Thanks in part to her efforts, the struggle for racial equality finally became a national issue.

Some of Mrs. Roosevelt's ideas on these and other issues were unpopular. People who felt threatened by her proposals sometimes called her an idealist, a busybody, and even a **communist**. Despite the criticism of her work, she kept fighting for human dignity and equal treatment for everyone. By the time she died, Eleanor Roosevelt had become one of the most famous and admired women of the twentieth century.

Eleanor Roosevelt at a federally supported nursery school for African-American children in Des Moines, Iowa, 1936

CHAPTER 2

A LONELY CHILD FINDS AFFECTION

Anna Eleanor Roosevelt was the child of wealthy but unstable parents. Her father and mother had problems of their own and spent little time with their children. By the time she was ten years old, Eleanor was an orphan. There were few bright spots in her life until she met a demanding but encouraging teacher and began spending time with her friendly cousin Franklin.

Eleanor (far right) with her father and brothers

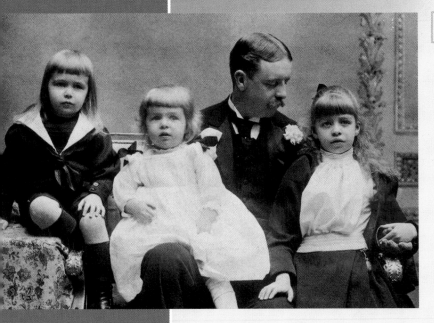

PARENTS

Elliott and Anna Hall Roosevelt belonged to New York City's upper class. They lived in a big house, had servants, and attended charity balls, polo matches, and other high-society events. Meanwhile, nannies raised their three children—Eleanor, Elliott Jr., and Hall.

Elliott Sr. was a charming, handsome man, but he was also troubled. As a child, he was less admired than his more successful brother, Ted; as an adult, he drank too much and accomplished little. Anna was beautiful but superficial. Her main interests were dressing well and entertaining. She did not give much time to her children.

EARLY CHILDHOOD

The Roosevelts' first child, Anna Eleanor, was born October 11, 1884. Eleanor was plain-looking, shy, and awkward—not the kind of child her beautiful mother had expected. Anna nicknamed her "Granny" and sometimes told her, "You have no looks, so see to it that you have manners." Ashamed and hurt by her mother's attitude, the little girl became even more self-conscious.

Eleanor's father was her favorite person in the world. Unfortunately, as his drinking got worse he acted badly and often spent months at a time in alcohol treatment centers. Finally, Anna separated from Elliott and took the children. Eleanor rarely saw her father after that, and she missed him terribly.

Years later, Eleanor Roosevelt said that she never smiled as a child. She also remembered having many fears—fears of the dark, dogs, heights, water, and being scolded. She once stated, "[I was] always afraid of something. . . . Anything I accomplished had to be done across a barrier of fear."

Eleanor's mother, Anna Hall Roosevelt, was a renowned beauty.

LIFE WITH GRANDMOTHER HALL

When Eleanor was eight years old, her mother died suddenly. Elliott could not care for the children because of his drinking, so Eleanor, Hall, and Elliott Jr. went to live with their grandmother, Mary Hall. Just a few months later, Elliott Jr. died of scarlet fever and diphtheria. Then, a year after that, Elliot Sr. also passed away. The ten-year-old girl was devastated, and she mourned the loss of her father for many years.

Eleanor at about age fourteen

"Ambition"

When Eleanor Roosevelt was fourteen, she wrote the following in an essay about ambition:

Of course it is easier to have no ambition and just keep on the same way every day and never try to do grand and great things, for it is only those who have ambition and who try to do who meet with difficulties and they alone face the disappointments that come when one does not succeed in what one has meant to do. . . .

Is it best never to be known and to leave the world a blank as if one had never come? It must have been meant, it seems to me, that we should leave some mark upon the world and not just live [and] pass away. For what good can that do to ourselves or others? It is better to be ambitious and do something than to be unambitious and do nothing.

Grandmother Hall was quite strict and took her responsibilities seriously. Wanting Eleanor to become a lady, she enrolled her in classes in music, dancing, and foreign languages and sent her to the theater and ballet. Sometimes she let her visit her father's brother, Uncle Ted, who would later become the twenty-sixth president of the United States.

ALLENSWOOD SCHOOL

When Eleanor was fifteen, she was ready for finishing school—a private girls' school that taught beautiful manners and social skills. Mrs. Hall sent Eleanor to a school in England named Allenswood. Allenswood was not a typical finishing school. Its founder, Marie Souvestre, wanted girls to get a real education. At a time when young women were encouraged to be dependent wives and mothers, Marie Souvestre challenged her students to use their minds, think for themselves, and act as responsible members of society.

Eleanor thrived at Allenswood and was popular with the other girls and her teachers. She and Souvestre went on trips through Europe, where the teacher encour-

Eleanor (one of the girls on the balcony) at Allenswood School in 1900

aged her to go sightseeing by herself and make travel arrangements on her own. These experiences were wonderful for Eleanor. She wrote, "For the first time in my life, all my fears left me."

Back at home, Uncle Ted's political career had blossomed, and in 1901, Theodore Roosevelt became the nation's youngest president. Eleanor liked her uncle, but she was not interested in politics, so the fact that he was president of the United States meant very little to her.

COMING OUT

In 1902, after three years in England, Eleanor returned to New York City to be introduced to society as a debutante. She attended fancy dinners, dances, and teas. Unfortunately, she did not enjoy them. She often felt lonely and self-conscious as she watched other girls chatting and dancing with their partners.

The only person who made these events seem like fun was Eleanor's distant cousin, Franklin Delano Roosevelt. A student at Harvard, Franklin was handsome, charming, and spontaneous. Best of all, he liked talking to Eleanor and said he admired her intelligence. When Franklin was at a party, she knew she had a friend there.

Fortunately for Eleanor, New York debutantes did not spend all their time at parties. They were also urged to help the needy by participating in various types of volunteer programs. Eleanor decided to join two volunteer organizations—the Consumers' League and the Junior League. Members of the Consumers' League investigated working conditions in clothing factories and department stores and refused to buy from businesses that mistreated employees. Since many employ-

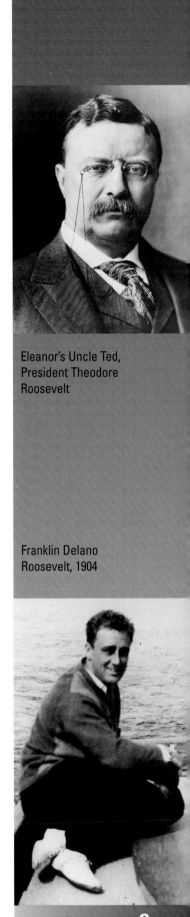

Eleanor's Uncle Ted, President Theodore Roosevelt

Franklin Delano Roosevelt, 1904

Working Conditions for Women and Children

In the early twentieth century, there were few laws governing labor, so cruel or greedy bosses could make workers' lives miserable. In many families, almost everyone worked—men, women, and children. Women and children were usually given the worst jobs in mills, factories, stores, and even mines. They often worked twelve- to sixteen-hour shifts in crowded, poorly lit rooms and unhealthy conditions. In New York City, wages for women and children were $.60 to $4.50 a day. Men were paid about $15.00 a day, but workers were fined when they made mistakes, so they often took home much less.

Concerned citizens protested the long hours, hard manual labor, poor working conditions, and starvation wages, but most bosses ignored the criticism. Change would come only when laws were passed that forced them to treat their workers better.

An eleven-year-old girl working in a hosiery factory, 1914

ers treated workers very badly in the early 1900s, Eleanor's experiences with the Consumers' League shocked her. She was particularly appalled when she saw four- and five-year-old children making artificial flowers, working "until they dropped with fatigue." Her assignment with the Junior League, however, was more fun. Working with that group, she taught dancing and exercise classes to poor children.

Unlike some of the young women in these organizations, Eleanor took her work seriously and was very troubled by the living and working conditions she saw. One day she showed Franklin the inside of a tenement (a run-down apartment building with very bad plumbing, heat, and light). Surprised and disgusted, he told Eleanor, "I didn't know human beings lived like that." Both Eleanor and Franklin were beginning to learn what it was like to be poor in America.

MRS. FRANKLIN D. ROOSEVELT

Eleanor and Franklin became engaged when he was twenty-one years old and she was nineteen. There was much for Eleanor to dream about and look forward to—a new home, as well as a loving life with Franklin, their children, and Sara, Franklin's mother. Things did not turn out as Eleanor expected, however. She tried to live up to her new family's expectations, but she often felt like a failure. Then she learned something about Franklin that made her feel even worse.

YOUNG WIFE AND MOTHER

Their wedding took place on March 17, 1905, with Uncle Ted standing in for Eleanor's father. A few months later, after Franklin completed his law degree at Columbia, the couple honeymooned in Europe. When they returned, they learned that Sara had purchased a house for them, three blocks from her own, in New York City. She had also furnished their new home and hired servants, so there was nothing left for Eleanor to do.

Sara Delano Roosevelt was a beautiful, strong-willed woman who was very close to Franklin. Eleanor and Sara wanted to feel close to each other, too, but their relationship was often difficult. Sara controlled Franklin's money, so she controlled the household finances. She also tried to manage the family's daily activities and was critical of Eleanor.

When the Roosevelts' first child, Anna, was born in 1906, Sara insisted that Eleanor stop doing volunteer work so she would not bring home "the diseases of the

Eleanor in her wedding dress, 1905

Eleanor's mother-in-law, Sara Delano Roosevelt, with Franklin and Eleanor

The Roosevelts in 1919—Franklin, his mother, and Eleanor on the top step; Elliott, Franklin Jr., John, Anna, and James seated below

slums." Eleanor didn't know much about children and felt very insecure about herself as a mother, so she accepted her mother-in-law's judgments and did as she was told. As the family grew to include five more children (one of whom died in infancy), Sara continued to rule the household in many ways.

Eleanor could not seem to please Franklin's mother, no matter how hard she tried. And Franklin was not much help. He usually avoided household friction and did not understand his wife's feelings. Eleanor felt worse and worse about herself and, as she put it, began "shutting up like a clam" and withdrawing from family activities. She even gave up learning to drive and play golf because Franklin criticized and teased her for making a few mistakes.

POLITICIAN'S WIFE

While Eleanor struggled at home, Franklin pursued his interest in politics. In 1910, he was elected to the New York state senate, and the Roosevelts moved to Albany, New York. Sara, however, stayed in New York City.

In Albany, Eleanor was away from her mother-in-law for the first time in six years. She hired her own staff, organized her own house, and made friends with other political wives. Since politics was Franklin's passion and she wanted to support his interests, she also attended senate debates and listened to informal political discussions when Franklin brought friends home for dinner. Eleanor was especially concerned about issues affecting education, poverty, and working conditions. She sometimes shared her opinions on these subjects with her husband, and he was impressed by her insights.

In 1913, President Woodrow Wilson appointed Franklin assistant secretary of the Navy. The Roosevelts moved to Washington, DC, where Franklin and Eleanor met and made friends with many people who were interested in politics on both the national and international levels.

After the United States entered World War I in 1917, Franklin traveled to Europe on government business and Eleanor sent the children back to New York to stay with their grandmother. With her family away, she was

Franklin Delano Roosevelt

The only child of wealthy parents, Franklin Delano Roosevelt was born in 1882 and grew up on the family estate in Hyde Park, New York. His parents adored him and gave him the best of everything. After he and Eleanor married, he remained very close to his mother and continued to have a special affection for his childhood home.

Franklin loved politics and was an ardent Democrat. He became governor of New York in 1929 and was elected U.S. president in 1932. He was the only president to be re-elected three times (1936, 1940, and 1944).

President Roosevelt's political skills and optimistic outlook helped him lead the country out of the worst economic crisis in its history—the Great Depression—and through most of World War II. While he was in office, the federal government set up relief programs to help the unemployed, created thousands of jobs, and provided support to struggling businesses. He is remembered as one of the most effective presidents of all time.

Like many other European cities and villages, the French town of Baccarat was nearly reduced to rubble during World War I.

once again free to do volunteer work. She worked twelve-hour days for the Red Cross, visited wounded soldiers in hospitals, and became a skilled fund-raiser. Convincing friends and government officials to make contributions, she raised money to build a physical therapy center for the wounded and obtained financial aid for soldiers who were disabled by their injuries. The work made Eleanor Roosevelt feel useful and happy. "I loved it," she later wrote. "I simply ate it up."

A CRUSHING BLOW

When Franklin returned from Europe in 1918, Eleanor found a packet of letters in his suitcase. Reading them, she learned that her husband was in love with an employee and close friend of the family—a woman named Lucy Mercer. This discovery was a terrible shock. Eleanor offered her husband a divorce; eventually Franklin promised to stop seeing Lucy, and the Roosevelts agreed to stay together. However, that decision did not end Eleanor's pain. In her own words, "The bottom dropped out of my own particular world, and I faced myself, my surroundings, and my world, honestly for the first time."

As the war ended, the Roosevelts worked to rebuild their marriage. They thought they needed to spend more time together, so, when Franklin was sent to Europe to close U.S. military bases in 1919, Eleanor went with him.

In some ways, their trip to Europe was like a second honeymoon. They enjoyed Paris, drove around other parts of France, and spent happy times with both new and old friends. The trip also had a grim side, however. Eleanor saw firsthand the real costs of human conflict— war widows dressed in black, ruined towns, and spoiled countryside that would take decades to recover.

Although the devastation in Europe was terrible, it helped Eleanor put her own troubles into perspective. Compared to the ruin she saw overseas, her personal and family problems began to seem manageable. She still felt insecure and depressed at times, but she began to realize that she needed to accept Franklin as he was and pay less attention to his life and more attention to her own. She decided that "life was meant to be lived and curiosity must be kept alive. One must never, for whatever reason, turn his back on life."

When this picture was taken in 1911, Eleanor was in charge of her own home for the first time in her married life.

CHAPTER 4

BECOMING MORE INDEPENDENT

Eleanor started looking for worthwhile things to do. Since she enjoyed volunteer work, she decided to join women's organizations that supported **liberal** causes she believed in. Through those groups, she made new friends, discovered that she had hidden talents, and began to feel that she could be useful to people whose lives and concerns were very different from her own. As Mrs. Roosevelt herself put it many years later, she began "drifting far afield from the old influences" and "thinking things out" for herself.

Eleanor and Franklin during his vice presidential campaign, 1920

LOOKING BEYOND HOME AND FAMILY

The struggle for personal independence began at home. First, Eleanor dismissed her white servants and hired an all-black staff because many African-American workers had lost their jobs when white men returned from the war. Then she started making important decisions about her children, and that led to many arguments with Sara. They seemed to disagree about most things—the children, politics, household finances, appropriate behavior, clothing styles, and more. But Eleanor now felt entitled to her own opinions, and she expressed them despite her mother-in-law's disapproval.

Meanwhile, Franklin's career was changing. In 1920, the Democrats chose

James M. Cox to run for president, and Cox asked Franklin to be his vice-presidential running mate. The two men campaigned hard but lost the election to Warren G. Harding and Calvin Coolidge. After that defeat, the Roosevelts moved back to New York City, where Franklin joined a law firm.

By this time, Eleanor was no longer willing to live her life solely through her family, so she began to look for work that would allow her to help other people. She soon joined the League of Women Voters, a new organization whose goals were to develop political power for women and promote such liberal causes as national health and unemployment insurance, federal aid to education, international peace, and the abolition of child labor.

Eleanor blossomed in this stimulating, supportive environment and became chairperson of the League's committee on national legislation. In that position, she evaluated congressional proposals that affected women, considered how the League might work to influence the final votes in Congress, and made recommendations. She also began making speeches. Terrified of public speaking, she had trouble at first, but with help from friends she became an effective and popular speaker.

The League of Women Voters was a controversial organization. Many **conservatives**, especially conservative men, sometimes said that the League's **progressive** ideas would destroy American families and weaken the country. But in Eleanor's opinion, "we can't be too conservative and [still] accomplish things," so she continued working with her new friends and supporting changes that she believed were fair, decent, and right.

Esther Lape (left) was a prominent member of the League of Women Voters. An independent, well-educated woman, she challenged and encouraged Eleanor (right) to work for social change. The two became close friends.

The Roosevelt home
on Campobello Island
in Canada

Franklin and Eleanor
on the beach at
Campobello, 1920

In 1921, an unexpected development forced Eleanor's focus to shift back to her family. While they were at the Roosevelt summer home in Campobello, Nova Scotia, Canada, Franklin contracted poliomyelitis, or polio. Polio is a serious disease that causes permanent paralysis. No one knew whether Franklin would ever walk again.

During the first three weeks of Franklin's illness, Eleanor slept on a couch in his room and cared for him in every way. Later, when Franklin's condition stabilized but he still could not move his legs, she and Sara disagreed over what he should try to do. Sara wanted Franklin to retire from politics and live an easy life, while Eleanor argued that he should exercise his weakened body and work on his political career. Franklin loved politics and wanted to continue in that field. Together, he and Eleanor finally convinced Sara that he could and should lead a normal, productive life.

NEW CHALLENGES

Though his recovery was slow, Franklin worked hard to regain strength and a bit of movement in his legs. Eventually, he bought a spa in Warm Springs, Georgia, where he often went to swim and relax.

Meanwhile, Eleanor became more politically active, partly to help Franklin stay informed and involved and partly to pursue her own love of politics and public service. She joined more political organizations, including the Women's Division of the Democratic State Committee in New York. Working with that group, she worked for better public housing, sanitation, and health care programs. She also influenced the New York legislature to pass laws to improve educational, living, and working conditions for children and women. Although some proposals that Eleanor publicly supported—such as the one reducing the standard workweek from 60 to 48 hours—failed to become law, her efforts made New Yorkers aware of social and economic problems that affected millions of people.

Eleanor began to urge other women to take charge of their lives and "gain for themselves a place of real equality and the respect of the men." She traveled, raised money, organized petition campaigns, debated, made speeches, and wrote magazine articles encouraging women to develop their own interests, enter politics, and work for economic change and world peace.

Eleanor Roosevelt, Nancy Cook, Caroline O'Day, and Marion Dickerman (seated) working together in New York, 1929

Women Working Together

In 1922, Eleanor met Marion Dickerman and Nancy Cook, two active and influential members of the Women's Division of the Democratic State Committee. The three soon shared a cottage on the Roosevelt property in Hyde Park, New York, started and ran a furniture factory, and co-edited the *Women's Democratic News*. They also bought the Todhunter School, a private school for girls.

Eleanor became the vice principal at Todhunter and taught classes in U.S. history, current events, and literature. Wanting every student to have "vivid, firsthand experience" and understand how all kinds of people lived, she took the girls to see police lineups, courtrooms, slums, and street markets. She also emphasized the importance of social responsibility and encouraged volunteer work.

Mrs. Roosevelt (shown above serving food to poor families) urged politicians to enact laws that would improve working and living conditions for women and children and ensure adequate health care.

Franklin, now widely called FDR, was elected governor of New York in 1928. By then, Eleanor held important posts in state and national organizations and was a political force in her own right. Her activities often made headlines in national newspapers, and people wrote letters to the editor about her work. Some people admired and supported her, but others considered her ideas to be dangerously un-American. No longer afraid of criticism, she continued her work.

When the Roosevelt family moved into the Governor's Mansion in Albany, Eleanor (now called Mrs. Roosevelt by nearly everyone who knew and respected her) was expected to attend teas, dinners, and other social events. She did what she had to but tried to spend most of her time doing work that seemed more important to her—teaching, giving lectures and talking on the radio, advising FDR on social issues, and urging him to appoint women to government posts. Because Franklin could not walk well, she also went in his place to inspect conditions in state prisons, hospitals, and public projects. After each inspection, she reported to him in detail.

In 1929, a severe economic crisis, known as the Great Depression, began in the United States and the rest of the world. Millions lost their jobs, their life's savings, and their homes. As governor of New York, Franklin set up programs to provide help to victims and offer long-term solutions to their economic problems. His work in New York put him in the national spotlight, which led to his nomination as the Democratic Party's candidate for president. With his election in 1932, he became the thirty-second president of the United States. His election presented new opportunities for social change—and new challenges for Eleanor Roosevelt.

CHAPTER 5

A NEW KIND OF FIRST LADY

Everyone expected Mrs. Roosevelt to give up her own work when FDR entered the White House. Historically, the president's wife stayed in the background, supervising social events while her husband did the country's work. Not Mrs. Roosevelt, though. She was determined to use her unique position as first lady to try to make America a better place for everyone. First, she traveled around the United States and learned about the lives and problems of people who did not receive much attention or help from the government. Then she came home, told both government officials and ordinary citizens what she had seen and how she felt about it, and urged them to help. For the twelve years of her husband's presidency, no matter how much she annoyed people (including, sometimes, FDR), she talked and wrote about these issues over and over again.

Mrs. Roosevelt's Firsts as First Lady

A very unusual first lady, Mrs. Roosevelt set many precedents. She was the first president's wife to give all-female press conferences; travel by plane; hold (and lose) a government job—Assistant Director of the Office of Civilian Defense; appear before a congressional committee; write a syndicated newspaper column; address a national convention; receive payment for lectures; be a radio commentator; and publicly disagree with her husband's policies.

TRAVELER AND COMMUNICATOR

When FDR took office in 1933, the country was in the worst economic depression in history. Concerned about the millions who were out of work and determined to learn about their problems firsthand, Mrs. Roosevelt began to travel widely. She visited and spoke with coal

President Franklin D. Roosevelt (center) entering the White House in 1933 with Eleanor and their son James

In 1935, the first lady (left) toured coal mines to learn about the conditions in which miners worked.

A Boy and His Rabbit

Eleanor Roosevelt once described a poor family she had visited. There were six hungry children and almost no food—only "the kind you or I might give a dog." Three of the children were standing in the doorway, and the youngest boy was hugging a white rabbit. Mrs. Roosevelt recalled, "It was evidently a most cherished pet. The little girl was thin and scrawny, and had a gleam in her eyes as she looked at her brother. Turning to me she said: 'He thinks we are not going to eat it, but we are,' and at that the small boy fled down the road clutching the rabbit closer than ever."

Rural poverty: the wife and children of a sharecropper in Washington County, Arkansas, 1935

miners, women, youth, African Americans, Native Americans, migrant workers, immigrants, and others who were still not receiving help through the **relief and reform programs** that President Roosevelt initiated to solve the country's economic problems. She also encouraged people to write to her about their lives and views. Hundreds of thousands of people did just that, and through their letters Mrs. Roosevelt learned even more.

Armed with the information she gathered through her trips and correspondence, she sent notes and talked to FDR and his staff every day. She explained how miserably some people lived and asked her husband and his aides to create programs and policies that would improve living and working conditions for these neglected groups of people. Some government agencies were eager to work with Mrs. Roosevelt on her causes. Through those agencies, she helped bring education, work, health care, and improved living conditions to the needy.

Mrs. Roosevelt shared her experiences with as many ordinary Americans as possible. In 1935, she began writing a daily column, "My Day," that was carried by newspapers nationwide. For the next twenty-seven years, this column allowed her to share her concerns with Americans everywhere. She also gave speeches, wrote books and magazine articles, and talked on the radio. In every way she could think of, the first lady publicized the problems she saw and encouraged people to think of imaginative solutions. "It is nice to hand out milk and bread," she said. "It gives you a comfortable feeling inside. But fundamentally you are not relieving the . . . reason why we have to have this charity."

Eleanor Roosevelt addressing the annual convention of the American Red Cross, 1934

Her schedule was filled with appointments and work activities for sixteen to twenty hours each day, and her energy amazed almost everyone. Few people realized that the first lady needed to be busy. When she was not working for and with others, she felt lonely, depressed, and unhappy. "Work," she once wrote, "is always an antidote to depression."

National Youth Administration (NYA)

In the 1930s, young adults faced many problems. There were few jobs for them and little training, and their needs had been overlooked by FDR's relief and reform programs. Mrs. Roosevelt was very concerned. She urged her husband to create a program that would serve young adults—women and men, black people and white, those in cities and those in the country. Largely because of his wife's influence, FDR created the National Youth Administration in 1935. Offering job training and educational opportunities to all young people regardless of race, sex, and location, the NYA was among Mrs. Roosevelt's greatest triumphs. She served as its advisor until it was dissolved in 1943.

In the 1930s, many African Americans lived in slums, such as this one in Washington, D.C. The U.S. Capitol can be seen in the background.

One group that particularly drew Mrs. Roosevelt's attention was African Americans. There had been amendments to the Constitution that gave all races equal protection under the law (1868) and the right to vote (1870), but those changes meant little to most black citizens. All over the country, and especially in the South, they were discriminated against at work, kept out of white communities and public places, and given little real protection under the law. Forced to live and work in unhealthy and inhumane conditions, many black Americans were poorly educated, starving, and desperate.

Mrs. Roosevelt fought hard for racial equality and integration. As she put it, you "can have no part of your population beaten down and expect the rest of the country not to feel the effects from the big groups that are underprivileged." She urged FDR to end discrimination in all federal aid and relief programs, encouraged the appointment of capable black men and women to government posts, and set up meetings between African American leaders and the president so they could discuss racial issues. In 1935, thanks largely to his wife's influence, FDR signed an order forbidding racial discrimination in the Works Progress Administration (WPA), the largest federal jobs program of his administration.

Mrs. Roosevelt's Changing Attitudes about African Americans

As a girl and young woman, Eleanor Roosevelt was raised to have a kind but condescending attitude toward African Americans. Much later, when her husband became president and she began traveling around the country, she supported the idea of racial equality and fought for the rights of black people. Even then, however, she still occasionally used words like "darky" and "pickaninny." When black Americans pointed out that those terms were offensive to them, she realized that she was not quite free of the attitudes she had learned in childhood. After making those very public mistakes, Mrs. Roosevelt became a more sensitive partner in the fight for racial equality and integration.

By inviting Marian Anderson to sing at the Lincoln Memorial, the first lady took a public stand against racial discrimination. Thousands attended the free concert.

Eleanor Roosevelt knew how to draw attention to her causes. In 1939, she attended the Southern Conference for Human Welfare in Birmingham, Alabama, and was told she could not sit with an African-American friend. Refusing to sit in the whites-only section, she picked up her chair, moved it into the aisle between the blacks and whites, and sat there for the entire conference.

On another occasion, the Daughters of the American Revolution (an exclusive women's organization whose members have traced their ancestry back to the American patriots of the Revolutionary War) would not let the famous African-American singer Marian Anderson perform at their auditorium. Mrs. Roosevelt resigned her membership in protest and set up a concert for Anderson at the Lincoln Memorial. Seventy-five thousand people attended.

Mrs. Roosevelt's views on racial justice were years ahead of most Americans', so some of her efforts failed. One of these failures involved efforts to pass an anti-lynching bill. Lynching, the killing of someone accused of a crime without a fair trial, was fairly common in America in the 1930s. In fact,

Eleanor Roosevelt goes to prison

An advocate of prison reform, Mrs. Roosevelt sometimes visited and inspected federal prisons. Once when she was out of the White House and had forgotten to tell FDR about her plans, he asked her secretary where she was. The secretary checked the first lady's calendar and told him, "She's in prison, Mr. President." "I'm not surprised," FDR replied, "but what for?"

eighty-three black men were lynched during FDR's first term in office. Mrs. Roosevelt strongly supported an anti-lynching bill and urged her husband to make lynching a federal crime. Unfortunately, FDR knew that his support of the bill would anger powerful white Southerners whose help he would need in other areas, so he refused. No federal law against lynching was ever passed.

Mrs. Roosevelt's support of the anti-lynching bill and other controversial causes upset some people. "If you have any influence with the president," one woman wrote to FDR's secretary, "will you please urge him to muzzle Eleanor Roosevelt and it might not be a bad idea to chain her up—she talks too damn much." That kind of pressure did not work with President Roosevelt. "You can say anything you want," he told his wife. "I can always say, 'Well, that is my wife; I can't do anything about her.'" With FDR's support, Eleanor Roosevelt continued to act on her beliefs that lynching is wrong and that every human being has the right to live in decency and dignity.

Many people who opposed integration were angered and appalled when a magazine printed this picture of Eleanor Roosevelt and a young black girl in 1935.

INTERNATIONAL CONCERNS

While the United States was struggling with economic and social problems, other countries began to suffer in even greater ways. Governments led by **dictators** were replacing democracies in Europe and taking away the people's civil rights. When Germany, Italy, and Japan invaded nearby countries, another world war seemed likely.

In the 1920s and 1930s, most Americans were isolationists, that is, they didn't want to get involved with other countries and their problems. Mrs. Roosevelt did not share their opinion. She thought the United States should work with other countries for world peace and the good of all people. Concerned about what was happening in Germany and elsewhere, she criticized the European dictators. She also urged the United States to participate in the League of Nations and the World Court, two international forums where issues between countries could be discussed and resolved without starting another war. In Mrs. Roosevelt's opinion, "America, by some form of cooperation with the rest of the world, must make her voice count among the nations for peace."

Her ideas were unpopular, and even when Britain and France declared war on Germany in 1939, the United States tried to stay out of the war. When Japanese warplanes bombed the U.S. naval base in Pearl Harbor, Hawaii, on December 7, 1941, however, staying out of the war was no longer possible. The United States entered World War II, fighting with Britain, France, and the **Soviet Union** against Germany, Italy, and Japan.

Adolf Hitler, the German dictator whose army opposed Britain, France, the Soviet Union, and the United States in World War II

U.S. ships burning after the Japanese surprise attack on Pearl Harbor, 1941

CHAPTER 6

FOCUSING ON PEOPLE DURING WWII

After the United States entered World War II, many Americans concentrated on military victories and losses, but Eleanor Roosevelt did not. As usual, she focused on people. She continued to actively support the needy in the United States, fought against racial discrimination in the armed forces, and encouraged both wounded men in hospitals and troops going into battle.

CONTINUING THE FIGHT FOR HUMAN RIGHTS AT HOME

During the war, many American women began performing jobs that had been considered men's work. Below, a woman welds a part for a bomber in 1942.

Although she was concerned about the war effort, Mrs. Roosevelt continued to work on the issues of poverty and inequality at home. In 1941, she influenced FDR in his ordering of defense industries to give African Americans a fair chance to work. As unremarkable as that may

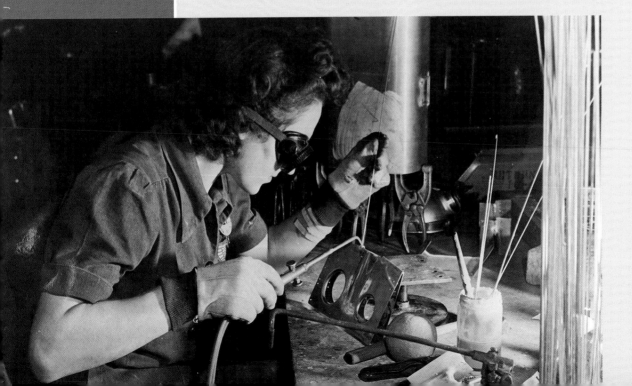

seem today, that order represented stunning progress for black Americans. In fact, the *Negro Handbook* called it "the most significant move on the part of the Government since the Emancipation Proclamation."

The first lady also continued to fight for women's causes and was delighted to see women by the thousands working while the federal government provided day-care facilities for their children. Many women had the opportunity to work in defense factories because so many men were in the Armed Forces. Women did so well that one executive said, "We may have thought a year ago we could never get along with them. Today we know we can never get along without them."

Some of Mrs. Roosevelt's efforts at home were less successful, including her attempt to preserve the civil rights of thousands of Japanese Americans. After Japan bombed Pearl Harbor, many people thought that all Americans of Japanese descent were threats to national security and should be treated as enemies. Mrs. Roosevelt argued that, since Japanese Americans were U.S. citizens who "were not convicted of any crime," they were still entitled to their freedom, their homes, and their jobs. Despite the first lady's arguments, President Roosevelt soon signed an order forcing more than 100,000 people to leave their homes in California and parts of Washington, Oregon, and Arizona. Taking only what they could carry, Japanese Americans moved to camps surrounded by barbed wire and stayed there for the next few years. Their confinement still stands as one of the worst wholesale denials of human rights in recent U.S. history.

Japanese Americans standing in line at an internment camp in Puyallup, Washington, 1942

When the United States joined the war, the nation's armed forces were completely **segregated** by race. White and black soldiers were grouped into different units, housed separately, and given different recreational facilities. Furthermore, white troops performed the preferred jobs, while black soldiers were generally not allowed to fly airplanes, participate in combat, or distinguish themselves in any way. Instead they were expected to cook, clean, serve the officers' meals, shine shoes, and perform other menial tasks.

Mrs. Roosevelt believed that "the basic fact of segregation . . . warps and twists the lives of our Negro population [and is] itself discriminatory." Consequently, she strongly objected to the separation of black and white soldiers and the preferential treatment given to whites. She talked and wrote about these issues at every opportunity, always trying to develop public and political support for fairer treatment.

Slowly, Mrs. Roosevelt's efforts and those of many others began to pay off. In 1943, the War Department forbade the segregation of military recreational facilities. The next year, the government outlawed segregation on federal trucks and buses. Finally, late in the war, African Americans were allowed to fly, and black

Mrs. Roosevelt pinning a medal on an African-American soldier, 1943

soldiers were asked to live and fight alongside whites. Even though black Americans continued to be oppressed at home, many African-American men were not only willing but eager to fight for the United States. Little by little, the armed forces were becoming integrated.

TOURS OF BRITAIN AND THE SOUTH PACIFIC

In 1942, President Roosevelt sent his wife to England to inspect U.S. bases there. During that trip, Mrs. Roosevelt saw the results of German bombing in London, made public appearances, and traveled to Red Cross clubs and army camps all over the country. She met and talked with thousands of U.S. soldiers and took messages home to many anxious families. Every evening, she wrote to or spoke with FDR to tell him what she had seen, what people had said, and how she felt. And she continued to write her daily newspaper column, "My Day," so she could share her impressions with the American people. "Every soldier I see is a friend from home," she wrote, "and I want to stop and talk with him whether I know him or not." When Mrs. Roosevelt returned to Washington, she had worn through the soles of her

No Sanctuary for the Jews

Prejudice and discrimination against Jews was never as extreme in the United States as it was in Europe. Nevertheless, **anti-Semitism** was common during Eleanor Roosevelt's childhood, and she shared that prejudice for many years. By the early 1930s, however, several of her closest friends and coworkers were Jewish. Then, in 1935, she learned that the **Nazis** were persecuting Jews in Germany. Given her usual outspokenness against social evils, it is surprising that she remained silent about the situation in Germany. Not until 1940 did she finally speak and write about what was happening there. Then she began arguing for changes in immigration laws to make it easier for European Jews to come to the United States, but her efforts came too late. The next year Hitler stopped letting Jews leave Germany. Because no country—not even the United States—opened its door to European Jews while they were still free to travel, millions died in the **Holocaust**. That disturbing truth did not escape Mrs. Roosevelt. According to her son James, her failure to help large numbers of Jewish **refugees** before and during World War II was "her deepest regret at the end of her life."

Mrs. Roosevelt talking with U.S. female ferry pilots serving in the Air Transport Auxiliary during World War II, 1942

shoes, exhausted the reporters who followed her, and become a celebrity in England, where her concern, sincerity, and kindness had meant as much to the British people as it had to American soldiers stationed overseas.

In 1943, Mrs. Roosevelt toured the South Pacific for a month. The trip did not start out well, in part because Admiral William F. Halsey, the officer in charge of the region, did not want to use important military equipment and men to help a civilian visit dangerous places and talk with the soldiers. After seeing how much her visit improved the men's morale, however, he changed his mind. He later said that Eleanor Roosevelt "had accomplished more good than any other person, or any group of civilians, who had passed through my area."

Despite the success of those trips, many Americans

Talking to Soldiers on Their Way to a Battle

When Mrs. Roosevelt went to the South Pacific during World War II, she wanted to spend time with as many soldiers as possible. One day, her group was traveling from one base to another when they saw a convoy in the distance. The first lady insisted on catching up. A reporter later wrote that she walked down the rough road, "her shoes dusty and scarred by rocks," and stopped at every truck to offer words of encouragement and thanks to hundreds of men who were preparing to fight and, perhaps, to die. "At one point," the reporter wrote, she found it difficult to control her emotions and "her voice quavered, but she quickly recovered and continued on down the line." She tried to talk with every soldier in the convoy.

still objected to their unusual first lady. They thought she should stay home, support her husband, and take care of the White House rather than travel without him and promote such controversial causes as integration and equal treatment of women on the job. In late 1943, a national poll showed that Eleanor Roosevelt had become "the target of more adverse criticism and the object of more praise than any other woman in American history."

U.S. marines preparing to advance on the enemy from behind sandbags in the South Pacific, 1943

Mrs. Roosevelt with a wounded soldier in the South Pacific, 1943

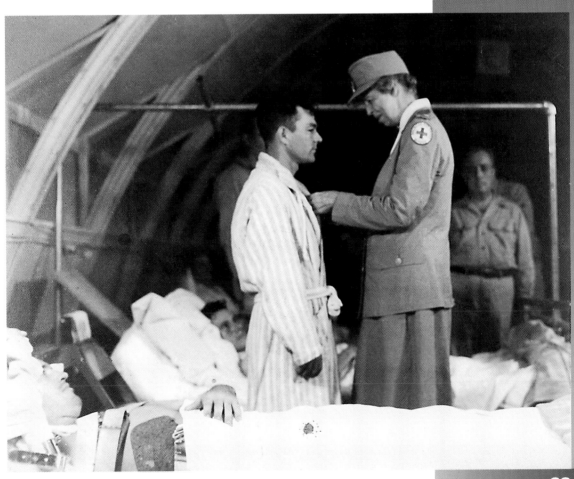

DEATH OF A PRESIDENT

In 1944, FDR ran for a fourth term and won, but his health was failing. He had begun to suffer from heart disease, he was easily fatigued, and his hands trembled. The general public was not informed of the president's health problems, but friends and family were quite concerned. Finally, in late March 1945, he went to his spa in Warm Springs, Georgia, for a two-week rest. The first lady stayed in Washington.

On April 12, 1945, while in Warm Springs, the president suddenly collapsed and died. Mrs. Roosevelt was notified immediately. Before leaving Washington for Georgia, she asked the vice president to come to the White House. There she told him that FDR was dead and that he, Harry Truman, was soon to be sworn in as the new president. Stunned by the news, Truman strug-

President Franklin Delano Roosevelt's funeral procession, Washington, D.C., 1945

President Harry Truman and Mrs. Roosevelt leaving her husband's funeral

gled to speak; finally, he asked if there was anything he could do for her. Knowing the problems he would face as president, she replied, "Is there anything we can do for you? For you are the one in trouble now."

Arriving in Warm Springs, Mrs. Roosevelt got another shock when a relative told her that Franklin's old lover, Lucy Mercer (who by that time was the widowed Lucy Mercer Rutherford), had been with the president when he died. As painful as it must have been to hear that news, Mrs. Roosevelt showed no emotion. Instead, she sat alone with her husband's body for a few moments and then began preparing for his funeral.

A train bore the president's casket and Mrs. Roosevelt back to Washington. Along the way, thousands of people lined the tracks to say goodbye to the man who had led them out of the Depression and through most of World War II.

Upon FDR's death, Harry Truman became the thirty-third president of the United States.

Eleanor Roosevelt returned to New York City after the funeral. There she expected to lead a quiet, private life. With her famous and powerful husband dead, she thought no one would care about her or her activities. So, although reporters surrounded her when she first arrived in New York, she rebuffed them. "The story," she said, "is over."

CHAPTER 7

THE MOST FAMOUS WOMAN IN THE WORLD

Mrs. Roosevelt was wrong—the story was far from over. In 1945, and again in 1961, she was appointed U.S. representative to the **United Nations (UN)**. There she worked for social justice worldwide and helped write the Universal Declaration of Human Rights. She often said that the work she did for the UN was the most important work of her life. In her later years, people everywhere admired her. The lonely, fearful child had become one of the most respected and powerful women in the world.

Right to left,
Eleanor Roosevelt,
Adlai Stevenson, and
John Foster Dulles at
the United Nations in
New York City, 1946

WORK WITH THE UNITED NATIONS

In December 1945, Mrs. Roosevelt received a call from President Truman. A new international organization was being formed to promote peace and security throughout the world; would she be interested in being one of five U.S. delegates? Despite her concern that she was not qualified for the job, Mrs. Roosevelt accepted the appointment and agreed to attend the first organizational meeting of the United Nations.

Eleanor Roosevelt had almost no experience in foreign affairs and was the only woman in an assembly of many men. Years later, she reflected, "I knew that as the only woman, I'd better be better than anybody else. So I read every paper. And they were very dull sometimes, because State Department papers can be very dull. And I used to almost go to sleep over them. . . . But I did read them all. I knew that if I in any way failed, it would not be just my failure; it would be the failure of all women."

She was right about how she would be perceived. Some of the other delegates, including those from the United States, were scornful and condescending at first. After Mrs. Roosevelt faced challenges graciously but firmly in several difficult meetings, however, those delegates realized she was a skilled debater and leader. One delegate later told her, "We did all we could to keep you off the United Nations delegation. . . . But now we feel we must acknowledge that we have worked with you gladly and found you good to work with."

Her work at the UN organizational meetings so impressed President Truman that the following year he appointed her to a more permanent position as the U.S. representative to the UN's governing body, the General Assembly. That group set up several important committees, one of which was the Human Rights Commission. Eleanor Roosevelt was unanimously elected the commission's chairperson.

Mrs. Roosevelt and the Human Rights Commission had an important job to do—

Excerpts from the UN's Universal Declaration of Human Rights:

Article 1.
All human beings are born free and equal in dignity and rights. They are endowed with reason and conscience and should act towards one another in a spirit of brotherhood.

Article 3.
Everyone has the right to life, liberty and security of person.

Article 4.
No one shall be held in slavery or servitude. . . .

Article 5.
No one shall be subjected to torture or to cruel, inhuman or degrading treatment or punishment.

Article 7.
All are equal before the law and are entitled without any discrimination to equal protection of the law. . . .

Article 9.
No one shall be subjected to arbitrary arrest, detention or exile.

Eleanor Roosevelt holding a Spanish translation of the Universal Declaration of Human Rights, 1949

Facing page:
Eleanor Roosevelt (center) with Nikita Khrushchev (right), his wife, and Soviet Foreign Minister Andrei Gromyko at the FDR Library in Hyde Park, 1959

write an official UN statement explaining the basic rights to which every man, woman, and child in the world is entitled.

Drafting this important paper took over a year. Many countries had no concept of human rights, and there were long arguments in many languages over what the statement should cover and exactly how it should be worded. Mrs. Roosevelt worked long days as she led the commission's struggle to understand and accept differing viewpoints and reach agreement on one issue after another. Finally, at approximately 3:00 in the morning on December 10, 1948, the General Assembly passed the Universal Declaration of Human Rights. That declaration still stands as the UN's most sweeping statement of the fundamental rights and freedoms to which all human beings are entitled.

TRAVELING TO PROMOTE PEACE

Mrs. Roosevelt resigned her official UN post after six successful years. She then began traveling widely at home and abroad to promote the UN and encourage commitment to worldwide peace and human dignity. She traveled as a private citizen but was so famous and respected that she was treated like a visiting head of

Mrs. Roosevelt and the Soviet Premier

In 1957, during the era of Cold War hostilities between the United States and its rival superpower the Soviet Union, the *New York Post* asked Mrs. Roosevelt to visit the Soviet Union and report on her impressions of life there. During her trip, she met Nikita Khrushchev, the Soviet premier. They discussed important issues and found that they had very different opinions on most of them.

Two years later, Khrushchev traveled to the United States and visited New York. While he was there, Mrs. Roosevelt invited him to tea. Her invitation upset Americans who thought it was wrong to entertain the nation's enemy. To Mrs. Roosevelt, that sort of thinking was too narrow. She said, "How, I wonder, do these people feel that we can learn to live together—as we must—if we cannot sit down over a cup of tea and quietly discuss our differences?"

Mrs. Roosevelt with Indian women in Bombay, India, 1952

Israeli Foreign Minister Golda Meir presents an award to Eleanor Roosevelt in 1961. Meir served as prime minister of Israel between 1969 and 1974.

state everywhere she went—India, Israel, Japan, Greece, Chile, Norway, the Soviet Union, and many other countries.

In between overseas trips, she was busy at home. She campaigned for political candidates, worked for civil rights, wrote, and lectured. She even hosted radio and television shows with two of her children, Anna and Elliott. In 1961, President John F. Kennedy appointed her to the UN again. He also asked her to chair the National Commission on the Status of Women.

During these years, Eleanor Roosevelt received many awards for her work as a **humanitarian**. She was often called "the greatest woman in the world" and voted "America's Most Admired Woman."

Eleanor Roosevelt—In her Own Words

I think we had better begin to decide whether we wish to preserve our civilization or whether we think it of so little use that we might as well let it go. That is what war amounts to.

The time to prepare for world peace is during the time of peace and not during the time of war.

If you care for your own children, you must take an interest in all, for your children must go on living in the world made by all children.

You gain strength, courage, and confidence by every experience in which you really stop to look fear in the face. You must do the thing which you think you cannot do.

Sooner or later we are going to realize that what touches one part of the human race touches all parts. Thus we are going to have to learn that the few must sacrifice for the good of the many if we are to preserve our present civilization.

LAST DAYS

Mrs. Roosevelt maintained her hectic schedule and wide range of activities until the spring of 1962, when she began to feel tired and suffer from aches and fevers. Her doctor eventually diagnosed the cause as a rare form of tuberculosis.

Although she was often bedridden and sometimes hospitalized over the next few months, Mrs. Roosevelt continued to see friends and work with

Eleanor Roosevelt and John F. Kennedy, 1960

her secretary. And she did not lose her zeal. Dictating to her secretary one morning, she said, "This I believe with all my heart. If we want a free and peaceful world, if we want to make the deserts bloom and man grow to greater dignity as a human being—*we can do it*!"

Eleanor Roosevelt died a few weeks later, on November 7, 1962, at the age of seventy-eight. She was buried next to her husband in Hyde Park, New York.

LEGACY

Eleanor Roosevelt was a great humanitarian, **reformer**, and diplomat. Adlai Stevenson, the U.S. ambassador to the UN at the time of her death, praised her contributions with these words: "What other human being has touched and transformed the existence of so many? . . . She walked in the slums of the world, not on a tour of inspection, . . . but as one who could not feel contentment when others were hungry. . . . She embodied the vision and the will to achieve a world in which all men can walk in peace and dignity."

A powerful voice for those who had no power, Eleanor Roosevelt is widely considered to have done more for social justice than any other woman in history. Nevertheless, the enormous problems she tackled—discrimination, hunger, poverty, and war—were not completely solved during her lifetime and are with us today. Her vision and her efforts to make that vision a reality continue to inspire people everywhere to work for world peace and human dignity.

"She would rather light candles than curse the darkness, and her glow has warmed the world." (Adlai Stevenson upon learning of Eleanor Roosevelt's death, 1962)

TIMELINE

1884	Anna Eleanor Roosevelt is born on October 11 in New York City
1894	Becomes an orphan
1899	Enrolls in Allenswood School
1905	Marries Franklin Delano Roosevelt on March 17
1906	Gives birth to Anna, the first of six children
1918	Learns that Franklin is in love with Lucy Mercer
1921	When Franklin becomes paralyzed from polio, encourages him to continue his interest in politics
1926	Purchases Todhunter School with Marion Dickerman and Nancy Cook
1928	Directs the Bureau of Women's Activities for the Democratic National Committee
1933	Becomes first lady when Franklin takes office as president of the United States
1934	Supports anti-lynching legislation; helps create the National Youth Administration
1939	When forbidden to sit with African Americans at the Southern Conference for Human Welfare, protests by placing her chair between the black and white groups
1945	Becomes a widow when Franklin dies on April 12; is appointed U.S. delegate to the United Nations
1946	Chairs the UN's Human Rights Commission and begins writing the Universal Declaration of Human Rights
1961	Is reappointed to the UN; chairs President Kennedy's Commission on the Status of Women
1962	Dies of tuberculosis on November 7

anti-Semitism: prejudice against Jews

civil rights: basic rights belonging to every citizen; in the United States, these include freedom of speech and religion, equal protection under the law, and freedom from slavery and discrimination

communist: someone who supports state control of the economy and equal sharing of land, materials, and products

conservatives: people generally opposed to rapid change and tending to want to maintain traditional views and conditions

dictators: rulers who hold absolute control

Holocaust: the massive slaughter of Jews by the Nazis around and during World War II

human rights: basic freedoms to which everyone is entitled, such as freedom of thought and expression and rights to life, liberty, and equal justice

humanitarian: someone who cares about the well-being of all people

integration: bringing people of different races together as equals

liberal: open to new ideas, especially political or social ideas; broad-minded

Nazis: members of the political party founded in Germany in 1919 and led by Adolf Hitler from 1933 to 1945

progressive: in favor of or working toward social change or reform

reformer: a person who fights social injustice and works to improve living or working conditions

relief and reform programs: FDR's programs that helped people and businesses recover from the Great Depression.

refugees: people who go to another country to escape danger or persecution for political beliefs, race, or religion.

segregated: separated on the basis of race or background into different neighborhoods, work groups, schools, churches, and public facilities

Soviet Union: communist country that existed from 1922 to 1991 in Eastern Europe and Northern Asia; included Russia, the Ukraine, and other member republics that are now independent nations

United Nations (UN): an international organization whose purpose is to maintain worldwide peace and security

TO FIND OUT MORE

BOOKS

Dash, Joan. *We Shall Not Be Moved: The Women's Factory Strike of 1909.* New York: Scholastic, 1996.

Doak, Robin. *Franklin D. Roosevelt (Trailblazers of the Modern World).* Milwaukee: World Almanac Library, 2002.

Freedman, Russell. *Franklin Delano Roosevelt.* New York: Clarion Books, 1990.

Freedman, Russell. *Eleanor Roosevelt: A Life of Discovery.* New York: Clarion Books, 1993.

Olson, Lynne. *Freedom's Daughters: The Unsung Heroines of the Civil Rights Movement from 1830 to 1970.* New York: Scribner, 2001.

Winget, Mary. *Eleanor Roosevelt.* Minneapolis: Lerner Publications, 2001.

INTERNET SITES

The Eleanor Roosevelt Papers
www.gwu.edu/~erpapers/
For Eleanor Roosevelt's political writings and radio and television appearances.

Franklin D. Roosevelt Library & Museum
www.fdrlibrary.marist.edu
For biographical information and other interesting resources on Eleanor and Franklin D. Roosevelt.

My Day
www.pbs.org/wgbh/amex/eleanor/sfeature/myday.html
For full text of selected "My Day" newspaper columns by Eleanor Roosevelt.

National First Ladies Library
www.firstladies.org
For biographies of Eleanor Roosevelt and other American first ladies.

Universal Declaration of Human Rights
www.un.org/Overview/rights.html
Full text of the UN declaration.

Women's International Center
www.wic.org/
For biographies of famous women, information on the history of women in America, and other resources.

INDEX

47

About the Author

Jonatha Brown has a broad background in writing and editing, much of it as a free-lancer helping corporations develop interactive computer-based training programs. A native of Rochester, New York, Jonny holds a BA in English from St. Lawrence University in Canton, New York. She currently lives in Phoenix, Arizona, with her husband and two dogs. She is delighted to be taking a break from corporate life by working with horses and writing books for children.